TRUE CRIME

FAKES AND FORGERIES

John Townsend

www.raintreepublishers.co.uk
Visit our website to find out more information about **Raintree** books.

To order:
☎ Phone 44 (0) 1865 888113
▤ Send a fax to 44 (0) 1865 314091
💻 Visit the Raintree Bookshop at **www.raintreepublishers.co.uk** to browse our catalogue and order online.

First published in Great Britain by
Raintree, Halley Court, Jordan Hill, Oxford OX2 8EJ,
part of Harcourt Education.
Raintree is a registered trademark of Harcourt
Education Ltd.

Editorial: Melanie Copland and Sarah Chappelow
Design: Lucy Owen and Kamae Design
Picture Research: Hannah Taylor and Ginny Stroud-
Lewis
Production: Duncan Gilbert

Originated by RMW
Printed and bound in China
by South China Printing Company

ISBN 1 844 43809 0
11 10 09 08 07 06
10 9 8 7 6 5 4 3 2 1

British Library Cataloguing in Publication Data
Townsend, John
Fakes and Forgeries – (True Crime)
364.1'63
A full catalogue record for this book is available from
the British Library.

Acknowledgements
Alamy Images pp. **14** (Popperfoto), **22–23**
(MedioImages), **24** (Charles Sturge); Corbis pp. **title**, **4**
(Lowell Georgia), **5**, **7** (Bettmann), **8** (Bettmann), **8–9**,
12–13 (Bettmann), **14–15** (Rune Hellestad), **17** (Paul
A. Souders), **18–19**, **24–25** (Reuters), **26–27** (Richard
T. Nowitz), **28–29** (Sygma/Inst.Optique/Zoko), **28**, **29**
(Bettmann), **30–31** (Sygma/Yves Forestier), **31**
(Bettmann), **35** (Bettmann), **39** (both), **40** (Sygma/Vo
Trung Dung), **40–41** (Digital image © Orbis; original
image courtesy of NASA); Getty Images pp. **5**
(AFP/Saeed Khan), **6** (Hulton Archive), **9** (AFP), **11**
(Photodisc), **11** (Time & Life Pictures), **16** (Photodisc),
16–17 (Photographer's Choice), **18** (Photodisc), **20–21**
(Photodisc), **33** (Hulton Archive), **34** (Time & Life
Pictures) **37**, **43** (Photodisc), **44–45** (Photodisc);
Harcourt Education Ltd pp. **12** (Tudor Photography),
21 (Ginny Stroud-Lewis), **22** (Gareth Boden), **27**
(Tudor Photography); Mary Evans Picture Library p.
6; Profiles in History p.**10**; Science Photo Library pp.
13 (Robert Holmgren, Peter Arnold Inc.), **25** (Tek
Images), **43** (Pascal Goetgheluck); The Kobal
Collection pp. **5** (Paramount/Touchstone), **36**
(Dreamworks/Andrew Cooper), **42**
(Paramount/Touchstone); Topham Picturepoint pp. **5**,
32, **33**.

Cover photograph of a dollar bill under a magnifying
glass reproduced with permission of Getty
Images/Stone.

Every effort has been made to contact copyright
holders of any material reproduced in this book.
Any omissions will be rectified in subsequent
printings if notice is given to the publishers.

The paper used to print this book comes from
sustainable resources.

CONTENTS

Any words appearing in the text in bold, **like this**, are explained in the Glossary. You can also look out for them in the Word Bank at the bottom of each page.

Things are not always what they seem. You cannot always be sure. What is real and what is not? Take a close look at your money. Is it really what you think it is? It may be worthless!

Can you tell if new designer trainers are the real thing or just a cheap copy? Maybe it does not matter, so long as they look like the real thing. But how would you feel if someone copied your signature and pretended to be you?

Fooling people is a serious crime. In the 1700s you could be hanged for it!

WORD BANK
counterfeit copy made to fool people
deceive make someone believe what is untrue

FRAUD

Fraud is a serious crime that can cheat people out of huge sums of money. It is based on lies. Fooling people or businesses to get money from them is a growing crime. Fraud also means tricking people into believing something is real when it is not. Criminals **deceive** their victims to get rich.

Fraud can be:
- Forgery – falsely making or changing something. Forged documents and paintings trick people all the time. They are often called:
- Fakes – anything that pretends to be what it is not
- **Counterfeits** – copies of something made to fool someone. Rare stamps and coins are often copied and sold.

FIND OUT LATER...

Why do some people pretend to be someone else?

When is a painting not even worth the paint it is made of?

How do you know if a photograph is a fake?

Can you tell if these watches are real or fake?

---

forger someone who makes a false item and pretends it is the real thing
stocks wooden frame with holes to lock the feet or hands in

NOT WHAT IT SEEMS

A person claims to have found an old document. It is written in old English and signed: **Shakespeare**. The world goes wild. A piece of writing by one of the most famous writers has been discovered! Then handwriting experts get to work. Scientists test the ink and paper – and find out it is a modern-day fake.

There are lots of stories about Elvis...could he still be alive?

WORD BANK   **autograph** person's signature in their own handwriting

Imagine you had a letter from a famous film star – with an **autograph** on it. That piece of paper could be worth a lot. If the letter told secrets, it could be worth a fortune!

As soon as a very important person dies, all kinds of letters and papers appear. People want to buy anything written in that person's handwriting. The only one who can say for sure if it is real is no longer alive.

An expert **forger** can make something up, copy a signature, and pretend it is the real thing. Then they just have to sell it to someone who believes them.

ELVIS

Since the singer Elvis Presley died in 1977, there have been stories of fakes. Recordings, signed photos, posters, and other objects have sold for high prices. But many are fakes.

Elvis himself was affected by forgery. When he was 3 years old, his father went to prison for forgery. Some say the biggest forgery of all was Elvis's death. Many people believe he is still alive after faking his death to start a new life. Every day people say they see him.

They probably just see one of his many lookalikes. Just more fakes!

Man arrested for fake Kennedy papers, New York, 1998

Lawrence Cusack was charged with **fraud** for selling papers that he said were written by US President John F. Kennedy. Cusack cheated many people in the USA of up to US$7 million by selling letters and notes he said were in Kennedy's handwriting. They were all fakes.

President Kennedy was very popular. People wanted to believe they had something he had written.

Shakespeare very famous English writer of poems and plays. He lived around 1600.

FAKE DIARIES

Many world leaders write diaries. They note down important events and the decisions they make. Sometimes they write about their feelings and what happens in their private lives. Diaries of world leaders from the past can tell us a lot about history. They become **valuable** documents.

Imagine you found an old book that turned out to be the diary of a country's leader. Lots of people would want to read it. **Publishers** might pay you a fortune for it. Some **forgers** think it is worth making up diaries and saying they were written by important people long ago.

COOKING THE BOOKS

After the Second World War, diaries and letters appeared that were said to have been written by leaders who had since died. In 1957, two women wrote 30 books to look like the diaries of the Italian leader Mussolini (above). They heated them in the oven to make them look older. They fooled a lot of people.

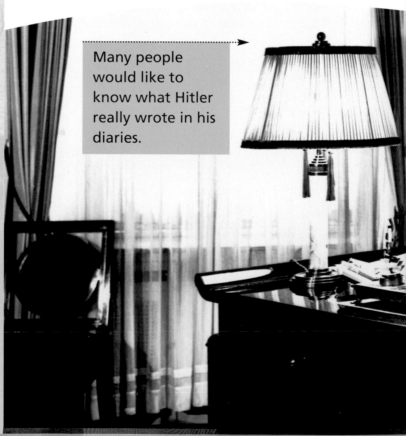

Many people would like to know what Hitler really wrote in his diaries.

WORD BANK

convicted found guilty of committing a crime
publishers people and businesses that make books

SELLING HITLER

In 1983, a magazine said it had 62 of Adolf Hitler's handwritten secret diaries. Hitler was the leader of Germany during the Second World War. It was said that Hitler sent his diaries away by plane for safe keeping in the war. The plane crashed, but someone saved the diaries from the flames. They kept them hidden for nearly 40 years.

The Hitler Diaries were called the most important discovery of the century. But in the end they turned out to be one of the biggest fakes of the century! Tests showed that the paper was just a few years old.

THE CULPRIT

A man called Konrad Kujau admitted to forging *The Hitler Diaries* and selling them. He had written them all himself, copying Hitler's handwriting. He was **convicted** of **fraud** and sent to prison for over 4 years.

Tests proved these diaries were a fake – but they fooled a lot of people!

valuable worth a lot of money

PHONEY LETTERS

Abraham Lincoln was president of the USA from 1861 to 1865. During this time he wrote many letters. Today most of his letters are kept in museums. Sometimes, though, a **dealer** will try to sell one of Lincoln's letters. If it is real, it is an important document and worth a lot of money. If it is a fake, it is worthless. So how can anyone tell?

Scientists can test the ink and paper. But **forgers** often use the exact type of paper and ink of the original document. Handwriting experts will also get to work. But a clever forger can sometimes fool them, too!

Do we really know that Lincoln wrote these letters?

BOGUS BOOK

Howard Hughes was a famous man. He was very rich and in the 1950s he lived like a celebrity. The world wanted to know about him. By 1970 he was an old man who never came out of his house. He became a man of mystery. Had he gone mad? Was he dead? Where was his money?

A writer called Clifford Irving wanted to cash in on the mystery. He wrote a book about Howard Hughes. He said that Hughes had helped to write it. Irving **forged** papers to hide his lies. When the truth came out, he was sent to prison for **fraud**.

WORD BANK   **dealer** person who buys and sells particular items

FEBRUARY 21, 1972

TIME

ON MAN OF THE YEAR

Clifford
Irving
by
Elmyr
de Hory

Special Section: A Guide to N

Clifford Irving became
a famous **con** man.

Fakes and forgeries
can lead to prison.

forger person who makes a false item and
pretends it is the real thing

11

FALSE WORDS

Imagine a rich old person died and left you all of his or her money. Some criminals do more than just imagine…

Eddie Adridge, from Speyside in Scotland, was jailed in 2004 for 18 months for forging the **will** of an elderly woman. Just before she died, he forged her signature on a false will that said she left £100,000 to him. Aldridge said he found the **will** at the woman's house. A handwriting expert showed that her signature had been forged.

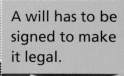

A will has to be signed to make it legal.

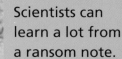

Scientists can learn a lot from a ransom note.

fibres tiny threads
forensic scientific investigation to help solve crimes

KIDNAP

Sometimes when a person goes missing, a **ransom** note is found. This usually demands money for the safe return of the missing person. But how can the police be sure the note is from the real kidnapper? Sometimes people try to make money by pretending to be the kidnapper and collecting the ransom. **Forensic** experts have to study each note. What do they look for?

Scientists can often tell how old a note is. They do this by examining the paper **fibres**. Sometimes marks on the paper can show where it was made and bought.

CLUES IN THE WRITING

Handwriting experts can match the writing from one document with writing from another. They look at:

- the shape and slant of the letters
- the thickness of the lines (to find the type of pen used)
- the spacing of words, the spellings, and **grammar**.

ransom payment for the release of someone who is kidnapped
will legal document to tell where someone's money goes when they die

13

SWINDLERS

DON'T BELIEVE IT!
Sellers have often told lies about themselves or the product they want to sell. Although this is **illegal** today, people used to say they were doctors so they could sell all kinds of medicine. In the 1880s in the United States "snake oil salesmen" went around selling a mixture they claimed could cure snake bites and many other illnesses. It could not!

Some people are not always who they say they are. They can be fakes. Would you trust anyone that knocked on your door? Every day people are **conned** by thieves telling them lies:

- they may say their car has broken down and they need to use your phone
- they may pretend to be a service engineer, saying they need to check your electricity or water
- they may work in pairs, with one doing the talking while the other slips in through another door of your house.

Elderly people are especially at risk from these kinds of thieves.

Would you trust this man?

WORD BANK   con to trick someone to get their money
footman servant who serves at meals or on a carriage

IMPOSTOR

An impostor is a person who pretends to be someone else to get what he or she wants. Sometimes they want to steal money or secrets. Newspaper reporters sometimes pretend to be someone else. They may even forge their **ID** papers so they can get a job, which allows them to spy on people to get a good story.

In 2003 a journalist for the *Daily Mirror* newspaper used false ID papers to get a job as the Queen's **footman**. He did this to show how bad the palace security was. Once inside he took many photographs, which were printed in the newspaper.

Con artists are tricking tourists into paying traffic fines. When they come home from their holidays abroad, victims receive important-looking letters. These warn them they committed a traffic crime when they were abroad and must now pay a fine. The con artists pick up the money when it is sent to a special address.

One of the Queen's footmen was nothing more than an imposter.

ID short for "identification". It shows who you are.
illegal against the law

IDENTITY FRAUD

Some people move to a new area and give themselves a new name, hoping to start a new life. They hope any problems from their past will be left behind. They might do this to stop someone finding them. They may be criminals who want to hide from the police. Sometimes they will steal another person's **identity** altogether. This could be by getting hold of a birth certificate of someone who has just died. Then they can use it to get a new passport and prove they are someone else.

Changing identity can be a way of escaping the police.

identity person's name and individual details
organized crime large gangs involved in crimes

CARS

The number plate on a car is like an identity tag that is linked to the person who owns the car. That is why criminals often change number plates or steal them from other cars. If the car is used in a robbery or if a speed camera catches it, the police will not be able to trace the criminals.

Police believe many stolen cars from Japan are being shipped to the UK and United States. This is part of a large **organized crime** operation. The cars are given new number plates and sold for a big **profit**.

A fake car is not always easy to spot.

CUT AND SHUT
Criminals sometimes fix together parts of crashed cars to make a "new" car. This is called "cut and shut". With just a little **forgery** to the car's papers, they can sell the car and make a lot of money. It is much safer to buy a car from a good garage that gets its cars straight from the factory.

PURE LIES

The Internet has given **fraud** a boost. There are a lot of fake websites offering all kinds of things. A fake email tells you that your bank has lost your details so you need to give them again. All a criminal has to do is make a website that looks like the real bank's website. This is called a **phish**. It tells people to type in their details, including their credit card numbers. Now the criminals have all the information they need to steal a lot of money.

FAKE DEGREES

Some students have used fraud to get qualifications:

- Cheating by saying another person's work is your own is fraud. It is called **plagiarism** and it is a crime.
- Some people forge or buy false exam certificates. The qualification is a fake, but some **employers** may be fooled by it.

invest use money to make a profit
phish an Internet fraud to get people's private details

PULLING THE WOOL OVER YOUR EYES

Beware of any advertisement that asks you to send money. Many people have been fooled into **investing** their savings into fake projects. Would you be fooled by an advertisement like this? It is the sort of fake that has tricked many people into parting with their money:

FAKE

Angora Geeps are a new breed that are turning the Australian wool industry on its head. The new fleece is fetching a high price in many overseas markets. We're looking for new investors. Profits are set to soar. For more information contact us quickly ...

FOOLED!
In 1998, newspapers and magazines across Australia showed fake advertisements. They were part of an April Fool's Day joke to warn people against fraud. More than 700 people were fooled into phoning for more information about investing in the fakes.

plagiarism   copying someone else's work and pretending it is yours

BIRTH, MARRIAGE, AND DEATH

Why would anyone get married to someone they do not know? There is big business in arranging this kind of wedding for **immigrants**. Once an immigrant is married to someone inside another country, he or she is allowed to live and work there. Getting married just for this reason is a crime called immigration **fraud**.

In the UK, there were thousands of marriage frauds in 2004. Many people were arrested. In the United States it is thought there are thousands of marriages arranged on the Internet each year. It is a way for many immigrants to get into a new country.

FALSE BIRTH

When a baby is born, it has to be **registered**. It is then given a birth certificate. At different times in our lives, we may be asked to show our birth certificate as **ID**. People who need to lie about their **identity** may end up forging a birth certificate.

Weddings can be fakes ... how can you tell?

WORD BANK   **green card** permit to live and work in the United States
immigrant settler in a new country

Man marries sixteen times in 1999

Manuel Febus admitted marrying sixteen women to help them get their **green cards**. When the police caught the 41-year-old New York man, he was sentenced to 5 years' **probation**.

He could have faced up to 5 years in prison for marriage fraud. He was given a lesser sentence because he helped police in other fraud investigations. Each immigrant woman paid Febus US$400 to be married to him.

FALSE DEATH

Every year there are criminals who fake their own death. They do this when they have committed a crime and are trying to escape from the police. They might leave a pile of clothes on the beach and disappear. They hope the police will think they have drowned. Meanwhile they run away to start a new life.

Criminals who fake their own death are almost always caught.

probation   punishment instead of prison, when behaviour must be good
registered   when details are written down in an official record

How nice it would be to have a machine that made money whenever you wanted it! Many criminals have thought of machines like this – and made them. They have printed their own banknotes. In fact, making false money is one of the oldest crimes. In the United States in the 1860s, about a third of all money was **forged**.

Even though we have colour photocopiers today, making forged banknotes is not as easy as you might think. Banks can soon spot fakes and can often trace where they came from.

SECURITY

Banknotes have special **watermarks** in the paper. These can hardly be seen until the note is held up to the light. They also have a security thread inside the paper. It shows up as a line when held up to the light.

Watermarks are difficult to forge.

mafia large organized criminal group

SUPER DOLLARS

In 1998, a criminal went into a UK bank to change a batch of US$100 bills into pounds. His 30-second visit began a huge police operation. The bills were all fakes. Detectives crossed the world on the trail of a very organized forgery gang. The "super-dollars" were the best copies ever forged. They even fooled experts. Police think the notes were printed in North Korea and then sent to Russia. The **mafia** have paid criminals around the world with the fake banknotes. Many have ended up in the UK.

MAKING FAKES
The paper in real US banknotes has tiny red and blue **fibres** inside it. Forgers try to copy them by printing tiny red and blue lines on their paper. Close study will show the lines on a fake are just on the surface – not inside the paper itself.

"Making" money the criminal way!

watermark a mark on paper that you can only see when you hold it up to the light

ON THE STREET

Computer software, scanners, digital cameras, and printers are a great help to criminals. These can help to make false documents such as tickets. Ticket **fraud** is a growing problem. Fake tickets for football games, pop concerts, or trains are being made. If you buy one, you will find your seat is already booked!

Buying from ticket **touts** can seem like a **bargain**.

Forger cost $500,000 (Canada, 2004)

More than 300 people were arrested when 20,000 fake subway tickets appeared in Toronto, Canada. The police caught a criminal gang printing thousands of travel tickets to sell at half price. The TTC plans to make its tickets harder to **forge**.

New York law

It is illegal to sell (or buy) tickets on the street for more than 10 per cent above the ticket price. Beware of people outside an event asking, "who needs tickets?" This is called "ticket scalping". As well as being expensive, tickets are often fakes!

WORD BANK   **bargain**   something on sale at a low price

PLASTIC FRAUD

Someone can pay for something by credit card on Monday and have no money in the bank by Friday. Huge bills could be coming in from around the world even though the credit card owner has never left home. It is all because of criminals "skimming" the credit card. This is when someone takes a credit card for a few seconds and swipes it in an **illegal** skimmer device. This copies all the information stored on the card's tape. The skimmer is so small it can be worn on someone's belt. Then a fake card can be made and used to buy anything.

Credit card fraud can happen in the blink of an eye.

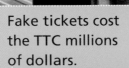

Fake tickets cost the TTC millions of dollars.

SELLING FAKE GOODS

Most people like a good **bargain**. But if you buy something that seems too good to be true, it probably is! You may not be buying a **genuine** product. It might be poor quality, or even dangerous.

Computers and the latest printers let criminals make false logos for stolen goods. Police estimate that up to 10 per cent of perfumes in markets are fakes, along with 12 per cent of toys and sports goods. Police raids have found that some fake perfumes contain **urine**! Bright coloured drinks have contained anti-freeze. Fake tea bags have been found full of metal filings, floor sweepings, and even mouse droppings. So remember – cheap goods are not always a good bargain!

PAYING FOR RUBBISH

If you are buying CDs or DVDs, look out for any with poor quality labels or covers. Check the wrapping is sealed. They might be cheap, but the quality will be poor. Fake CDs can rob musicians of huge amounts of money.

Look out for people selling fakes from market stalls.

genuine the real thing – not a fake
seize find and take

RISKY

Illegal and fake car parts are being sold all the time. The police often **seize** fake brake pads and discs. These, and fake steering parts, could easily fail and cause terrible crashes. Cheap does not mean safe. With car parts it can be very difficult to spot a fake. Criminals can copy the design and logos of genuine parts. But the materials they use are different and below safety standards. It always pays to check.

WARNING

Even if a fake is safe and of good quality, would you want to buy it? Buying **counterfeit** goods can cause more harm than people think. You could be giving money to **organized crime.**

Think twice before buying fake goods – do you know where your money is going?

FAKE TREASURES

People pay to see very old treasures and pay even more to own one. **Relics** are old objects that people believe are linked to religious leaders from long ago. They are so rare and **valuable** that some people fake them.

THE SHROUD

For hundreds of years, **pilgrims** have gone to see a piece of cloth called the Shroud of Turin. It has the mark of a face on it. It was said to have wrapped the body of Jesus Christ. Recent tests showed the cloth was not old enough. It was a fake made years after Jesus died. Even so, some people still believe the shroud is real.

HOLY OBJECTS
An object from long ago can be of interest to millions of people today. There are many pieces of old wood on display around the world. They are said to come from the cross of Jesus Christ. But if they were all put together they would make a forest!

Is this the face of Jesus, or just a big fake?

WORD BANK glaze shiny surface on pottery
pilgrim person who travels to a place for religious reasons

THE MISSING THUMB

Between 1915 and 1921 the Metropolitan Museum of Art in New York, USA, bought three large statues. They were thought to be 2500 years old. But in 1960 it was found that they were fakes! Their black **glaze** had material in it that was never used in ancient times.

One of the **forgers** was Alfredo Fioravanti. As an old man, he admitted he had made the statues. He even produced one of the statue's missing thumbs to prove it!

THE SKULL OF MYSTERY
Piltdown man was one of the most famous **frauds** in the history of science. In 1912 Charles Dawson said that he had found a skull in the Piltdown quarry in Sussex, England. It was said to be millions of years old. It was half ape, half human – the missing link between humans and apes. Forty years later it was found to be a big fake.

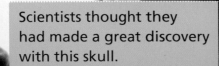

Scientists thought they had made a great discovery with this skull.

relic old object thought to be linked to a holy person

COINS AND STAMPS

Collectors pay a lot for rare coins, so **forgers** try hard to make good fakes. It is not always easy to tell if coins are **genuine**. This is because ancient coins were made by hand, so no two coins were **identical**. Expert coin dealers in New York, USA, were fooled into buying many fake ancient coins in 1999. Later they discovered them to be forgeries.

Machines make today's coins. Fake coins are often made by pouring liquid metal into moulds. This sometimes leaves cracks or pimples of metal on the fake coin.

Real coins are made by machines like this.

gummed coated with glue for sticking on to paper
identical exactly the same or equal

Collectors also buy stamps. If a forger can make a stamp that looks just like a very rare one, they could make a lot of money. The Penny Black was the world's first **gummed** postage stamp. It was printed with black ink and cost a penny. About 68 million of these were made in the 1840s in the UK. There could be over a million of them in collections today. Some will be fakes. A used Penny Black can sell for £75 or so. An unused one is rare and can sell for over £2000. That could be worth a forger making a few.

US STAMPS

In 1847, the USA issued its first stamps: a 5-cent stamp showing Benjamin Franklin and a 10-cent stamp with George Washington. Fakes have been sold to dealers. In 2004 one stamp dealer bought US$80,000 worth of fake US stamps.

This was the first US stamp.

PAINTINGS

You may dream of finding a **valuable** old painting in the loft. Or what if you bought a cheap painting at a sale and it turned out to be a lost masterpiece? All your money worries would be over.

Some criminals try to fool people by painting a picture and pretending it is by a famous artist. Artists have been copying other artists for thousands of years. In fact, copying the **old masters** is often part of an artist's training. But some students have got too good at copying. They realize they can make a living from it.

John Myatt at his trial.

old master painting by one of the famous artists from the past

THE ART OF CRIME

Two British men, John Drewe and John Myatt, made millions of dollars from selling fake paintings before their arrest in 1995. For 10 years, Drewe sold **forged** paintings to art galleries. He forged the records and papers of great paintings then paid Myatt, an artist, to copy the works of art. The copies and forged papers fooled many art experts. The director of New York's Museum of Modern Art said it was one of the biggest art **frauds** ever. Both men made a lot of money – before ending up in prison.

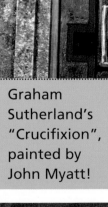

Graham Sutherland's "Crucifixion", painted by John Myatt!

> If the **counterfeit** is a good one, I should be delighted. I'd sit down straight away and sign it.

Picasso – a great 20th century painter (above) whose paintings are often forged.

Some **con artists** are in a league of their own. Their whole lives are spent fooling others. They might make a lot of money from crime to begin with… but does it last?

ELMYR DE HORY

A few artists prefer to copy paintings rather than make up their own. Elmyr de Hory **forged** about a thousand classic paintings. He was born in 1905 in Hungary. When he moved to the United States, he became the world's biggest art **forger**. Now other artists copy his fakes! A **genuine** Elmyr de Hory fake can sell today for over £10,000.

FOOLING THE EXPERTS

Elmyr de Hory forged and sold paintings that he claimed were by Henri Matisse, a famous French artist. One of the forgeries was sold to the Fogg Art Museum at Harvard University, USA.

Elmyr de Hory was a famous faker.

WORD BANK   **con artist** someone who cons people

A LONG CAREER

Elmyr de Hory was famous around the world as a talented artist. He took great care over detail and fooled most art experts. He sold his clever forgeries for high prices. In fact some of them sold for the same price as the original, even though the buyer knew they were fakes. Despite going to prison, he kept at his criminal career for about 30 years. He made a lot of money to begin with, but his life did not have a happy ending. His money ran out. Like some of the artists he copied, Elmyr de Hory became poor and eventually killed himself.

Orson Welles fools the world that aliens have arrived.

genuine the real thing – not a fake

CATCH ME IF YOU CAN

Even as a boy, Frank Abagnale used to lie, cheat and **con** others. When he ran away from home he began to **defraud** banks. For 2 years he posed as a Pan Am pilot. He had no idea how to fly a plane, but he wanted to travel around the world for free. He got hold of a uniform and **forged** an **ID** card. He would simply turn up at the airport desk and say he needed a ride. He billed all his food and lodging to Pan Am. He was so convincing that everyone believed him. Luckily, he was never actually asked to fly a plane!

DiCaprio met the real Frank before he started filming.

As well as forging a **diploma**, Frank forged cheques for US$2.5 million. He needed a lot of money to support his lifestyle! He cheated people all over the United States and was wanted for **fraud** around the world.

When he was 21, someone in France recognized Frank from a wanted poster. He was arrested and put in prison for 5 years. Then he was sentenced to another 12 years in the United States. But in 1974, the FBI offered him a deal. They would release him if he would advise them on fraud. He agreed and now helps to fight crime rather than commit it.

Today Frank fights crime by spotting fakes and forgeries.

diploma document proving a person has finished a course of study

JUST A LAUGH?

Sometimes a fake is harmless fun. Just a bit of a joke. But do not be tempted!

ONLY A HOAX

It might start off as a bit of fun. A practical joke is meant to make someone laugh. But it can all go wrong if a hoax involves **fraud**.

A hoax is meant to fool people... but sometimes it can go too far and become a crime.

Secret Service question boy over fake banknotes (Alabama, USA, 2004)

Secret Service agents called on a US schoolboy after he made US$10 bills for his class. The boy printed the bills on a simple printer and handed them round in a lesson. A friend tried to spend one at a local shop in Clarke County, Alabama. The shop owner spotted the fake and called the police. The **forger**, who only made the bills as a joke, ended up in big trouble.

Any threat to a country's money is seen as a serious crime.

WORD BANK hoax joke, trick, or something that is not real

FAKE POLICE

Fancy dress can get you into trouble. If you want to pretend to be a police officer to play a trick on someone, it is wise to think again!

Youth arrested (Wenatchee, Australia, 2004)

A teenager could face charges of **impersonating** a police officer. He faked being a traffic cop. The 17 year old stopped a female motorist and said she had made an **illegal** turn. He asked for her licence and went back to his truck, where he spoke into a pretend radio. When he returned, he told her it was all a joke. She noted his number plate and called the police. They did not see the joke!

Pretending to be a police officer is a serious offence in most countries.

A real police road block in Australia.

BEFORE YOU DRESS UP...

When a person is found guilty of criminal impersonation, it is also an act of forgery. You are committing a crime if you falsely take the **identity** of someone to harm another person or make something for yourself. It is not worth being a fake!

FAKE PHOTOS

Do you believe what you see? We used to believe that photographs showed the truth. But some people even wonder if images of great events were faked.

In July 1969, Neil Armstrong was the first man to stand on the Moon. He was seen on televisions around the world as he planted the US flag on the Moon's surface. Or did he? A very few people think it was all a **hoax**. They look at the photo of the flag and ask:

- Why does the flag wave when there is no wind on the Moon?
- Why are there no stars in the sky?
- Why do the shadows look so strange?

CHANGING THE TRUTH

People used to say that the camera never lies. But now we know it can. Today it is easy to "airbrush" an image on a computer. It can be done to make someone look a bit different. It may be done to make a joke picture. Or it might be done for a criminal reason.

This fake photo was made to show the Loch Ness Monster in Scotland, UK.

WORD BANK   staged set up

HOAX OR CRIME?

Does it matter if people make fake photos? Is it really a crime? We expect to believe what we read in a newspaper. We also expect to believe what we see. But sometimes a photo might be made up or **staged**.

In 2003, a reporter for the *New York Times* resigned when it was discovered that he had been faking most of his stories. He had pretended to be reporting from cities all over the United States, when in fact he was in New York all the time. He had made everything up!

SPOTTING A
FAKE PHOTO

Shadows
Shadows under noses and eyes should fall in the same direction. The lack of shadow can also be a clue.

Edges
Sometimes an image has been cut and pasted. Look closely for marks around the edges.

Repeats
If a photo has two or three objects that look exactly the same, it is likely they are copies. It is rare for many things to look identical in real life.

A few people believe that photos like this are fakes.

Never before have the faces of so many people been fake! New noses, cheeks, and chins, or facelifts to get rid of wrinkles, can change our looks forever. It is not just done to look good, either. Many criminals have plastic surgery so the police will not spot them. Even a forger's face could be a fake!

Fakes and **forgeries** will always be used to trick people for fun. But they are also part of a growing crime. It is likely that you or someone you know will be a victim of forgery or an act of **fraud.** Three out of five people in the United States are victims of forgery. It has a high cost:

- fraud costs US organizations more than US$400 billion each year
- the average company loses about 6 per cent of its total income to fraud carried out by its own workers.

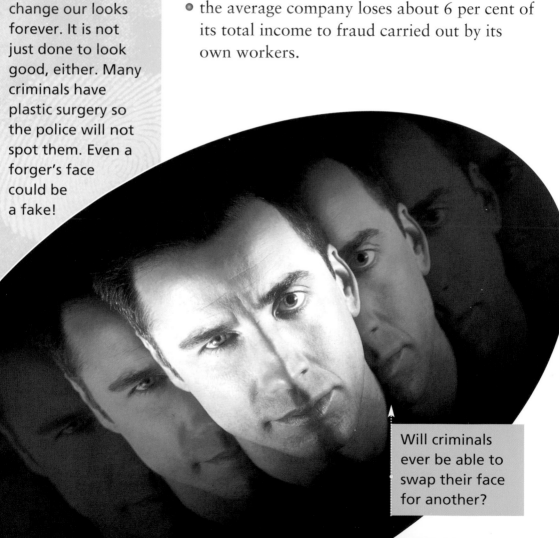

Will criminals ever be able to swap their face for another?

DNA code in each person's genes inside their body
hologram three-dimensional picture made by reflected light

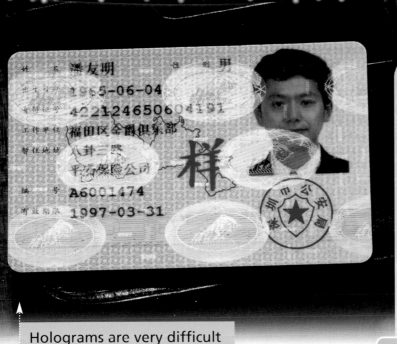

Holograms are very difficult for forgers to copy.

FIGHTING FRAUD

More and more forgers are getting caught. New technology may help their crime, but it also helps the police to catch them. There are now better ways to stop fraud:

- special security paper for documents. This can have **holograms** and advanced bar codes that cannot be changed or copied.
- **laser** inks that glow under special lights
- microchips and **PIN**s to stop credit card fraud.

One day every person may have to carry an **ID** card with his or her **DNA** information on it. That might upset a few criminals. Or will they find a way to forge those, too? We shall see.

Photocopiers are useful – but they can be used for crime.

laser very strong, fine beam of light
PIN Personal Identification Number

If you want to find out more about the criminal underworld, why not have a look at these books:

Behind the Scenes: Solving a Crime,
Peter Mellet (Heinemann Library, 1999)
Forensic Files: Investigating Murders,
Paul Dowswell (Heinemann Library, 2004)
Forensic Files: Investigating Thefts and Heists,
Alex Woolf (Heinemann Library, 2004)
Just the Facts: Cyber Crime,
Neil McIntosh (Heinemann Library, 2002)

FRAUD IS BIG BUSINESS
Nearly 2 million Americans may have been victims of **fraud** in 2004. The cost to banks and customers could be US$2.4 billion. That is an average of US$1200 per victim.

DID YOU KNOW?

- The last person to be hanged for **forgery** in England was Thomas Maynard, in 1829. Long before then, forgers had their ears cut off or their nostrils snipped. Ouch!

- Thieves build websites selling everything from sporting goods to contact lenses at bargain prices. The websites look very real. There could be between 800 to 1000 fake websites online at any time. They may only be there for a few hours but that is enough for victims to type in their credit card details. That is all the thieves need to steal the details to do their own shopping!

BIG LOSSES
In 2003, credit card fraud losses reached over £402 million. This was a result of theft, **counterfeiting**, and other types of card crime. About £30 million were stolen because the cardholders' numbers were copied from the cards themselves or from papers carelessly thrown away.

GLOSSARY

autograph person's signature in their own handwriting

bargain something on sale at a low price

con to trick someone to get their money

con artist someone who cons people

con trick (short for 'confidence trick') method of conning someone

convicted found guilty of committing a crime

copyright legal right to copy and sell something

counterfeit copy made to fool people

dealer person who buys and sells particular items

deceive make someone believe what is untrue

defraud cheat someone out of money

diploma doument proving that a person has finished a course of study

DNA code in each person's genes inside their body

employer someone who pays people to work for them

fibres tiny threads

footman servant who serves at meals or on a carriage

forensic scientific investigation to help solve crimes

forge to make a false item and pretend it is the real thing

forger someone who makes a false item and pretends it is the real thing

fraud fooling people or businesses to get money from them

genuine the real thing – not a fake

glaze shiny surface on pottery

grammar how sentences are put together

green card permit to live and work in the United States

gummed coated with glue for sticking on to paper

hoax joke, trick, or something that is not real

hologram three-dimensional picture made by reflected light

ID short for "identification". It shows who you are.

identical exactly the same or equal

identity person's name and individual details

illegal against the law

immigrant settler in a new country

impersonate pretend to be someone else

invest use money to make a profit

laser very strong, fine beam of light

mafia large organized criminal group

old master painting by one of the famous artists from the past

organized crime large gangs involved in crimes

phish an Internet fraud to get people's private details

pilgrim person who travels to a place for religious reasons

PIN Personal Identification Number

plagiarism copying someone else's work and pretending it is yours

probation punishment instead of prison, when behaviour must be good

profit when you sell something for more than you paid for it

publishers people and businesses that make books

ransom payment for the release of someone who is kidnapped

registered when details are written down in an official record

relic old object thought to be linked to a holy person

seize find and take

Shakespeare very famous English writer of poems and plays. He lived around 1600.

souvenir something that is kept as a reminder

staged set up

stocks wooden frame with holes to lock the feet or hands in

tout someone who tries hard to sell something

urine waste water you pass out of your body when you go to the toilet

valuable worth a lot of money

watermark a mark on paper that you can only see when you hold it up to the light

will legal document to tell where someone's money goes when they die

witness someone who is there when something happens

INDEX

Titles in the *True Crime* series include:

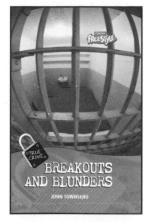

Hardback: 1844 438120

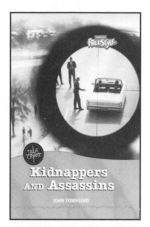

Hardback: 1844 438112

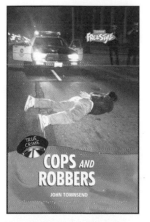

Hardback: 1844 438139

Hardback: 1844 438104

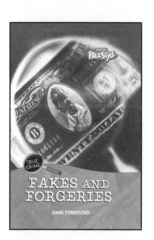

Hardback: 1844 438090

Find out about other Freestyle titles on our website www.raintreepublishers.co.uk